*walk softly please*

To Dave

# have i told you about my superpowers

*a book of resilient verse*

## LUTHER KISSAM V

Little Star ✷

To Dax

Published by Little Star
Richmond, VA

ISBN 978-1-7358872-5-8

### About the cover

Whether manic "sailing with planets" or using "the rust of mars" to describe anger, emerging poet Luther Kissam V draws on the celestial, the terrestrial, and sometimes the mundane to explore mental health. These elements push and pull Kissam's deeply personal poems through chaos and calm, meditations and medications, and ultimately, to balance. For Kissam, bipolar is a gift from the moon, a gravitational force, that fuels exploration of space: mental, physical and spiritual.
Cover illustration and book design by Wendy Daniel

Contact the author at www.lutherkissamv.com.

Contact the publisher at www.littlestarcommunications.com.

# Contents

## Lithium

# Lamotrigine

## Lithium & Lamotrigine: Maintenance

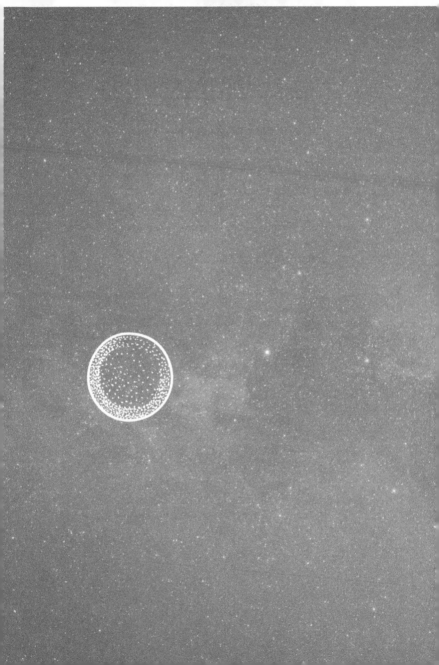

# Lithium

*Lithium (Eskalith, Lithobid) is one of the most widely used and studied medications for treating bipolar disorder. Lithium helps reduce the severity and frequency of mania.*

—WebMD

## poem in which I rhyme eight times because rhyming is fun

I am inevitably manic

sailing with planets

do not panic

rhyme is not satanic

it is only my antics

when I am awake damn it

mania is divine my own fanfic

bipolar I am it

# poem in which I attend a party

I am not even drunk

but I am the life

of the party

having danced

with every woman

in the building

because warm bodies

pressed against my

warm body excite

me and excitement

is the only reason

to party or even live

and no I reiterate

I am not even drunk

# poem in which I go on a tinder date

my hands have left marks on the steering wheel

they know each other well and the worn

leather melts into my skin I pull out of my driveway


the road is under construction

long chains of men work hard hours tonight

operating machines under giant lights

that illuminate the asphalt that they pancake

and pancake until it is level

I lean out the driver's window and yell

*what do you get paid?*

the wind swallows my curiosity

as I speed down I-85 I am not thinking clearly

I look past my headlights find exit 140 turn

my mind races like my car past the ants working

on the side of the interstate frantically carrying

grains of sand to build their castles

the working men flattened

the colony with the machines

the ants and I are starting over


I park see her silhouette through her window

she has a big smile wears glasses

I hope she is soft I have driven

ninety miles in the night to love a stranger

# poem in which I spend money I do not have

my mother read me a children's book

about giving bubblegum to rats

when I was a young boy the rat

never could get enough and eventually

if you gave a rat a piece of bubblegum

the bastard took your soul or something

like that since I spent a nickel

I've spent a dime and a dollar

and one thousand dollars

I did not know I needed six different

colors of the same nike sneakers

everything was golden

until now I have spent more dollars

than I have and my sticky fingers

are reaching into my mother's purse

and brother's wallet and maybe

even my roommate's piggy bank

if I spend another dollar

I will turn into a rat and chew

all the bubblegum I can find

even if it's my mother's or friend's or yours

## poem in which I write an incredibly long run-on sentence and an incredibly short sentence

who says calm is the enemy of creation

when it is clear that perfect is the enemy

of good for most folk—sad sad men

and women and queer persons

and children sweet sweet children

who imagine the world is their oyster

and every moment is new and raw

to them like sushi or a skinned knee

from scooter crashes on asphalt

because they could not land the jump

that seemed so monumentally large

but in reality was five or so inches—

but for us gifted folk good is our enemy

like guilty pangs reminding us of wrongs no

forgetting us of goods and yes

we gifted folk cannot create from nothing—

the blue ocean or the white

neutron star or the black hole sucking

in the milky way or maybe nothing

is the everything—but the entropy

of the universe yes the second law

of thermodynamics can birth einstein

in the same world as a heroin junkie

shooting up in a dirty alley

with a needle in their arm

unconscious but I think no one

is better than anyone else except

for me because I am simply better than

einstein and certainly a junkie

who robs banks and his own mother

for enough money to get high again

but truly I say unto you no man

or woman or queer person can

create anything of value from peace

and truly jesus said unto me

blessed are the insane and he holds

the most special place in heaven

for me and my gifts and truly I ask

does god in heaven himself believe

calm is the enemy of creation?


I do

## poem in which I complain about the state of the world

if I watch society swing to an extreme

again ostracize a person for their mistake

throwing them out with the trash and recycling

for the garbage gnats to crawl over

and lay eggs on I will spontaneously combust

and collapse into myself like a star

too massive for its own good


have you ever tried to be tranquil

in an increasingly extreme world? I'm told

*Tone down your intensity* at least twice a day

but do these motherfuckers not understand

my brain does not tone down on command?

I am a punch drunk fighter who has forgotten

how to use his inside voice but I can still deliver

a knockout for the ages I am the rust

on mars and I am as angry and agitated

as the seroquel will let me be which is to say

I am incredibly tired for six hour intervals

during the day before I return to the id

a celebrity did an unforgivable yesterday

I cannot even remember what it was


but I am no longer allowed to enjoy

their music and that movie they've been

producing the one I have been looking

forward to has been canceled by the studio

and twitter is disabling their account

as I write this and did you know I have

done worse when I am manic

or even just having a bad day did you know I'm

told to swallow weights for my brain so I cannot think?

# poem in which I try drugs

me&babe & lingo & greedy hands running candle wax over drying bodies

bodies of sinew tissue matter doesn't matter insignificance of beings

being a beam of sunset orange melt sinking through crust

crusty is the look I look at the eyes of the speaker

speaking in tongues through speakers stereos' basses

bass boosted to get our faces loosened for kisses

kissing with tongue like birdsnake my beak of a nose straightened

straight shiny teeth in a row me&babe & lingo & sneaky hands

hand paint & crawl on the floor crawl down my back

back it up back it up back back it up

## poem in which I practice radical acceptance at my psychologist's urging but it does not change my mood

it is a dbt skill
like mindfulness
or tipp to tolerate
distress and I am
distressed
right now
in the best way
possible

my eyes close
in his office
as I remind
myself to try
it so I whisper
*I don't like it*
*that's okay*
*I cannot change*
*it I can stand*
*it anyway*

but I cannot
stand it or I
don't want
to stand it
and would
much rather
perseverate
on my anger
until it consumes
the angel
sitting on my
shoulder
telling me to calm
down
I allow myself peace
for a moment

but only because my
psychologist
is a good man
and now that I
have calmed
myself to tranquility
I can see nirvana

isn't lack
of emotion
but control of it
and the ceiling
fan gently spinning
above could hypnotize
me if I let it
and maybe
maybe
my impossibly
agitated self
could let go
of the unfairness
the righteous anger
that burns
my insides
a furnace
consuming me
reducing my mind
to ashes

I am supposed to take long breaths while I repeat
my mantra *I don't like it that's okay I cannot change
it I can stand it anyway* but where is the fun

in that
in healthy stable

I refuse
a stable
reality

I cannot
radically accept
myself if I am
boring

*I like this*
it's great
I won't change it
I accept mania
I like this
it's great
I won't change it

# poem in which I attempt manic meditation

I am supposed to focus
on my breath or on a lotus

flower's patterns or even
a god that I do not believe in

I cannot try to still my mind
it races and races yet I feel fine

and the hypnotic nails
on a chalkboard propel me like sails

towards the other side of the sea
I keep my eyes closed picture teeth

glistening white biting
through tough meat I am writing

about the scale of things
the goodness of mary's wild geese

I am writing in my head
because I cannot find a lead

pencil to my liking and I am sick
of pens smearing their ick

onto my hands that are smooth
lotioned I am as uncouth

as a sailor I prefer music to poetry
but I cannot sing or grocery

shop or do anything useful
when I am in this state I'm truthful

to a fault so that I tell
my secret desire to sell

plastic shark's teeth to idiots
and I want drug dealing affiliates

the theme of my meditation
the chaos of this presentation

I heard I am supposed to focus
but I change my mind at a moment's notice

## poem in which I compile my social media posts from my current episode

is it just me or is today the most beautiful day

in the history of the world?


y'all ever think about the consequences

of a capitalist market driven foundation for policy

decisions?


shakespeare wishes he was as smart as I am


I don't claim to have the answers

but I'm just saying we should eat the rich


we should just kill racists


I am serious

rich people should starve too while we're at it

I want to drink gaga's bathwater

my mom just called me and said I needed
to chill I hung up on her

hi mom

they're coming for me

remember when they come for me
they came for jesus too because he spoke
the TRUTH

THE TRUTH WILL SET YOU FREE

## poem in which I resemble a man who has railed lines of cocaine for three days consecutively without sleep

*have I told you about my superpowers?*
the moon gave them to me
I am on fire but it does not hurt
it is only uncomfortably hot
so I have taken my clothes off except
my boxers because the world
is not worthy *are you trying to stop*
*me?* the moon told me you would
I can stop a car with my body
that is why I am racing towards
the highway you cannot stop
me I am the moon's warrior he
will smite you *See?* he is flying
down from space to kill
you because I asked him to
*am I okay?* of course I am
I have never been better

# Lamotrigine

*Recent findings have also illustrated the importance of lamotrigine in alleviating the depressive symptoms of bipolar disorder, without causing mood destabilization or precipitating mania.*

> —Prabhavalkar, Kedar S et al.
> "Management of bipolar depression with lamotrigine: an antiepileptic mood stabilizer."

# Poem in Which i Try to Apologize

i was manic, but i know that does not make
it okay for me to do the horrible i did.
My brain moved faster than my conscious,
and i know i said horribles and did horribles
and i'm somewhere between depressed
and manic now that i've started coming down,
and the only way i know to apologize
is to write this poem and clothe it in
sad, yellow apologies like *i'm sorry*
or *i will do whatever it takes to fix this.*

i fear the damage is done like the kindling
theory of manic episodes burning pathways
through my brain each time i'm like this.
Each time i'm like this. Each time i'm like this,

i always dig a hole that i can't climb out of,

and this time i'm so deep that no one will throw

me a rope, so maybe it is best for me

to apologize and mean it and not feel sorry

for myself because each time i choose

to enjoy this, i choose to go deeper.


The sad, yellow apologies

are crying, and perhaps i should tell

them i'm sorry for crying wolf all those times,

handing them out like candy on Halloween

when i didn't need to. Maybe, if i apologize

to my apologies they will stop being sad.

Maybe, if i say i'm sorry this time, i'll mean it.

# Poem in Which i Study Grief
## *after "Vulnerability Study"*

Running across campus for better cell
service to hear what i already do not believe.

Tears on a chapel's hardwood floor—swears at God.

Tears on a chapel's hardwood floor—prayers to God
to raise Lazarus again.

Calling the hotline on New Year's Eve
so i don't watch the ball drop alone.

Setting his favorite gift—tiny hands—in a tree
so he can watch the birds in the sky.

## Poem in Which i Grieve The Owl on 1700 West Broad

It watched from Joe's thigh. Its only eye
remained open to the world, eyelid hung
low. It saw too much at house party fight
pits that painted its black ink feathers blue.
They were crumpled like tissue paper.

i imagine if owls could smell it would wash
the must of weed and sweat off itself
by nose diving into a still, blue lake
from a red sandstone cliff. The ripples
would be tiny tsunamis because Joe flipped
from diving boards in high school.

But the owl had no nose, only a night-black
beak that struck in the sun and curved
downwards like a scythe. It melded
into Joe's thigh when he covered the owl

with his shorts so that only its inscribed

signature was visible beneath his pant leg

*1700 W. Broad* written in long script over his knee.


i cannot forget those sharp pointed

ears cocked back behind the owl's head.

They must have heard the grating metal music

and booming trap. Perhaps they only listened

to his quiet vibration—the foot thumpings

and anxious tremors. He told me,

"I tattooed wisdom on my thigh."


The owl flew back to its home on top

of *1700 W. Broad* when Joe died. i am

in Richmond to see my friend. i see

the bronze sculpture. The little owl that inspired

Joe's tattoo. It gazes over his cemetery

full of daffodils and lilacs. i bring a pale rose.


O little owl since my feathers are ruffled too,

will you shed a tear with me? For a moment.

# Poem in Which i Emulate My Least Favorite Poem
### *after "The Red Wheelbarrow"*

so much depends

upon

a plain bi-

polar

man with in-

sane

eyes beside the

children

# Poem in Which i Refuse to Answer My Phone and My Voicemail Inbox is Full

The saddest part
    is i have the energy
to answer and even talk,

    but i refuse to be
a burden on anyone
    anymore than i already

am. i know i am
    not a burden like
my brain knows

    it can control my breath,
but eventually, no matter
    how hard i try to hold

it, i breathe
        again. It is my grandmother
calling me this time.


        i know she will call me
back tomorrow. i can
        answer her then.


i have nothing to say
        to her or anyone who
would listen to me.


        My brain is empty,
dull like a used blade
        struggling to slice tomatoes.


The phone rings. Again.
        i wonder
if someone has died,

     or is ill or if today

is my birthday

       and i have forgotten.


The phone rings

      incessantly, and i

do not realize


     that i am worth

worrying about

     like the economy or weddings.

## Poem in Which i Take Seroquel on My Twenty-first Birthday

My head is heavy, and maybe it is the single

shot of tequila i took with my childhood crush

that sends the world spinning around me.

Perhaps i've had one too many

and my body is swaying, staggering, trying

to hold steady in the bar. To say i'm

overstimulated would be one of the great

understatements—like calling Cleopatra

decently attractive or Einstein's IQ above average.


i, for my part, do not think it is liquor

that lulls me to sleep, but rather the pills

which i have ingested only two hours

earlier. My doctor says i am having an episode,

and i know he is right and cannot pretend

to be naive anymore. i have been dealing

with this for too long. so the fifty milligram

tablet i swallowed is now drowning me in sleep.


i hear Bobby Shmurda rapping

over the bar's speakers, and the girls go crazy

when he hollers, acting as if he is here,

in the flesh. For a second, i contemplate

that he may very well be here and in my

inebriated state, i would never know.

i cannot hold a thought in my head,

but i do not want to be a party pooper.

Instead, i half-assedly rally, buy a pretty girl

a drink, fall asleep in the bathroom

until a drunk's banging on the door rouses me.

## Poem in Which i Dream i am Performing Hamlet

i am performing in an empty room. The audience

has already left, but i still know i am performing.

*All the world's a stage,* i think, but i

cannot remember the name of my mother

or father or uncle or Ophelia. i have forgotten

all my lines. i know it is my turn to speak

and feel the audience hold its breath

from impossibly far away, eyes boring

through me. i want Ophelia to hold me.

i want to hug my father. i want to murder

my uncle. It isn't fair. It's never fair.

The audience is still waiting, on the edge

of their seat. i do not know who i am

talking to in this scene. i do not even know

what scene i am in. *To be or not to be*

i am fumbling my words, *i know my answer*

and i am horrified for i have spoken the truth.

## Poem in Which i Listen to Loud Music Instead of Dying

Have i ever heard a bass like that?

One that wiggles my toes and bursts

my eardrums, and have i listened

so that i might feel the reverb in my testacles

reminding me of my manhood?

The lyrics are an afterthought

to the melody, and the melody is an afterthought

to the vibe, and have i ever considered

that maybe, to the universe,

the Earth is flat, just a meaningless point

on the scale of it all, of ever, of good

vibrations that palpate my prefrontal cortex?

Life is a rational choice because this song

playing is worth listening to again,

damnit, and again and again.

# Poem in Which i am so Depressed i Beg for Help

i miss the southern breeze

that gnaws at my memory while i ponder.

The northern chill pushes through my spine.

The Dr. says to wait and be realistic,

that becoming a zombie is a necessary price.

i swallow my tongue, breathe down my noise.


Do i feel alive despite the pained noise

my throat makes in the shower? The breeze

ices my wet hair, purples me. The price

of youth. At the Boxer Bikini Run we ponder

our mortality, our morality. If we're realistic

i am more than cold—winter lives in my spine.

November is dark, a skeleton, all spine,

skulless and toothless, deaf to the noise

of our adolescent, naked, never realistic

bodies hurtling through the snow, the breeze

sending shivers down our arms. We ponder

what love feels like when there is no attached price.


i am a husk waiting for reanimation. Life's price

is paid with unwashed sheets. My spine

aches. The flu tears at me, but i ponder

why i only feel sick when there isn't noise

to distract me. The Dr. says, "It'll be a breeze.

Your medications just need adjusting." i'm realistic.


December is for pessimism and no realistic

idealist can convince me otherwise. The price

of her kiss is my reputation. "Relax like the breeze"

our teacher says, "then pass my test." i circle my choice—spine.
We have learned about nerves in anatomy. My inner noise
begs, "What does it feel like to feel?" i ponder

why winter numbs me. The greats, too, ponder,
*why?* i only have enough energy to plagiarize. Realistic
goals. The end of the tunnel. The Dr. makes noise.
i cannot leave my room. Is this the price
of my creativity? Is it worth my spine
breaking in the cold? Brittle. i miss the southern breeze.

i miss noise. i can only ponder
why. The breeze is gone forever. "Be realistic"
"Dr." i respond, "Name your price. Take my spine."

# Poem in Which i Take my Mood Stabilizers

Reluctantly.

i come from another place.

i look in the mirror cup

of water in my right hand

a handful of pills cupped

in my left. i throw the cup

sending water flying. It is empty.

My hair was long before I buzzed

it. This time, it was to be as tranquil

as a monk. i hoped it would heal

me without the pills. My reflection

is still watching me. i do not like

the way it judges me.

i am thin. i have not had the energy

to eat for weeks. All i can do is sleep.

i hate myself and i don't understand

why a perfect God made

me so imperfect. i have been here before.


i stare at the pills in my hand,

tiny milligrams of Lithium

and Lamotrigine that will return

me to my room. i know they will kill

my darlings. i do not have water anymore.

i dry swallow them.

Reluctantly.

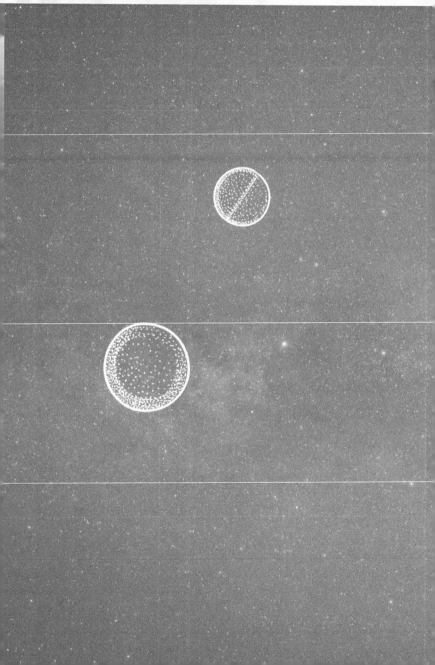

# Lithium & Lamotrigine: Maintenance

*Bipolar doesn't have to stop you from reaching*

*your goals, but it will take constant, vigilant*

*maintenance to manage it in order to meet them.*

> —Margot Brandi, MD, Medical Director
> of Sibcy House, Lindner Center of Hope

# Poem in Which I Psychoanalyze Myself

Repetition is the mother of learning.

                              In me,
there is still a young boy speaking in tongues
on the playground before school starts.
And even though my parents told me not to, I tell
fibs, stories, lies. I tell them to the teachers
and students and anyone else that will listen
but not believe me. I tell them Evan and Jim
and Caleb and Roger bully me. My friends—
even though I only have a few—believe.
Not always my fibs. But at least in me.

                              In me,
there is still a young boy wielding a stick
made of swords, fighting ogres and wizards
who rain fireballs down from dark towers. I dodge
them with ease, like the mosquitoes dodge me.
They bite me in the summer evening breeze,
too fast to squash with a slap and so their bites

become red welts that I scratch until they bleed.
"BLEED," I scream as my stick decapitates
my enemy. The violence of my youth.

                              In me,
there is still a young boy crying on stage
because second place in the school math
competition isn't good enough.
My parents are ashamed of my tears.
"Pick your chin up. Smile. Stop making
a fool of yourself. Of us. We raised you better."
They never believe when I say I was cheated.
Still don't. Another fib I told.

                              "Ms. Rollins
would never spite a fifth grader like you accuse.
She would never pick up your test first
and not give you the full thirty minutes
to finish. And even if she did, you shouldn't
have said math was too easy. If you were
as smart as you say you are, it wouldn't matter."

Anyway

she was my fifth grade math and science teacher.
My parents told me she had a good heart. They fibbed.
I remember what she told me, too.


"Strive

to be average. Just try to fit in. Don't ask so many questions."


She told the class repetition is the mother of learning.


"Strive

to be average. Just try to fit in. Don't ask so many questions."


In me,

there is still a young bully who singled out
John Sanchez. I cannot forget, cannot forgive
myself. I am ten years old, but I know
what I am doing. We all do. Find him
in gym class, the chubby one with the bowl cut,
grab the smallest ball I can find during dodgeball—

it hurts the most—and I peg him as hard
as I can with it. Aim for the face. Or the nuts.
Make it hurt.


                              In me,

there is still a young lover who kissed
his best friend. It isn't to him what it is to me.
For him, it is to win a bet. "See, we're still straight."
I tell another fib to Cameron in the bathroom
after he watches us kiss. My best friend is upset
when the gift card Cameron has promised us
has no money left on it. Cameron still can't believe
we actually did it. I can. When my friend says
we can't be friends anymore because I am changing
schools, I punch him. Aim for the face. And the gut.
Make it hurt.


                              In me,

there is still a young poet, writing in
the Valentine's cards we make for each other
in fifth grade. They aren't poems worth

remembering, but the burning of hot
glue on my fingertips is. I remember peeling
the hardened glue off like a molting crab,
a rattlesnake shedding its skin. I could see
my fingerprints in the mold. I couldn't feel
my fingerpads for a week afterwards.


                                        In me,
there is still a young boy in terrible pain.
Some of me died, the first time I tried to kill
myself. Soon I was sent to Utah. For wilderness.
More of me died there. They'll tell my mourning
mother they'd loved me for years if I die young.
They'll tell my mourning mother how they
all were robbed of years to come. I would tell
them all, if the dead could speak, I was robbed
of years that had already passed.


                                "Strive
to be average. Just try to fit in. Don't ask so many questions."

My parents never told me if they called the school.

"Strive

to be average. Just try to fit in. Don't ask so many questions."

Repetition is the mother of learning.

# Poem in Which I Think I am Truly Stable

Now that I am in the clear,
for now at least, and my mood
has steadied like a balanced
scale and the mirror smiles back
calmly, having wiped away
the wicked grin and the circled eyes,
I can sleep enough to rest.

I can dream a thousand gentle
moments and hold them tightly
against my chest like a child
might hold their teddy bear
when they're scared of monsters
beneath their bed, and yet,
despite my fear I will sleep
and sleep deeply until I awake refreshed
me again, stable, not distressed.

# Poem in Which I Defend an Incredibly Unstable Man from Judgment

Why should that man stay still when he can

talk to all his imaginations?

He should frolic under stars and dance

in the moonlight beneath God's constellations.

North and South are the same at the poles.

Polar bears kill seals. Penguins swim,

huddle together through ice and cold,

sitting on eggs they pray will live.

He cannot love a balanced scale

for that man has kissed the equator, bathed

in the Amazon, swam with whales

in warm waters, burned in the Sun's rays.

Why should he stop moving? He will

never be temperate, never be still.

## Poem in Which I Learn How Inosculation Feels

My psychiatrist is a kind woman, but no one
would mistake her for gentle. It's why I respect
her and her long, broad nose that fights
the mask the clinical directors make her wear.
I even like her despite the words she uses,
like a hammer, to smash the stories I've told
myself into a million fragments that I can
never piece back together. She makes me promise
I won't try. She begins in her Latino accent,

"People like you, and there are many happy,
successful people like you, need to take two mood
stabilizers and sometimes, like in your case, an extra
antipsychotic to help manage the mania. We use
Lamictal and therapy to treat the depression,
and the longer you stay stable, the more resilient
you'll be when an episode comes around."

She pauses. I brace for the hammer.

"You're also not as stable as you can be.
We're keeping you here in residential, increasing
the doses on your medications."

Her words are too much to process at once. I see
her hand push a pen across her prescription pad.
Her handwriting is elegant for a doctor. Her words
are a blunt instrument. There is nothing surgical
about psychiatry. I am afraid of the answer, but I still ask,

"How long will I need to take medications?"

"Forever."

I look out her window to avert my eyes
from her pad and nose and black hair
and medical books that are in English
and Spanish and past the resident
physician that joins our meetings.

My eyes catch two trees. They are joined
in the middle. Fused together in a memory
of when they first met. Still, they climb,
reach, touch the sky. My psychiatrist
catches my eyes wandering.

"In forestry, they call that inosculation.
The trees are colloquially known as gemels."

I wonder if she knows everything else
there is to know—Mandarin, how to bake
a cheesecake without cracking the crust,
and the secret to a happy marriage—considering
the authority she always speaks with. It angers
me. I feel powerless. Then I realize I know
something she cannot learn—how the gemels feel.
I laugh, tell her,

"Thank you."

# Poem in Which I Discover Euthymia

You're somewhere in the middle

between starving because I

don't have the energy to feed myself

and starving because I have too much

energy that eating would explode me.

You're neither a soft smile with an eyebrow

wag or the tears of sad frustration.

You're not good. Not bad. Without judgment.

Euthymia, you tortuous necessity!

I will love you.

# Poem in Which I Visit my Mind's Farm

The ducks are in a row.
The eggs hatch into the predicted number
of chickens. They only cluck
when spoken to.

The cornfields are always fertile.
Weeds never grow.
The rain only ever comes
when it's wanted.

The people who labor
never milk the wrong cows.
They never say stupid things
when they speak.

In my mind's farm,
I do not have to work.
I lose the farm
when I awake.

## Poem in Which I Love Because the World is Full of Beauty

The world is, after all, full of beauty and joy.

My niece was born yesterday afternoon,

and though I have not yet met her tiny feet

and held her in my arms to whisper, "Alora,

you're so, so beautiful," as she sleeps,

I already love her like I love the goodness

in the woman's heart who knits beanies for the babies

in the ICU. I love her like I love the kindness

in a granddaughter's soul as she changes her grandmother

who cannot remember her, and bathes

her despite the protests and dementia.

Have you seen the sun rise over the marsh?


It kisses the horizon so gently that mother Earth

warms us from the inside out. Like a newborn


that reminds me of love.

The world is, after all, full of beauty and joy.

# Poem in Which I Miss Someone

We talk to each other on the phone or through Zoom
on our laptops during the evenings when I have

access to my electronics. It is my most treasured
time of the week in this treatment center of hope.

Still, I want more: to reach out, place my hand
on her knee when she's hurting, notice her legs shake

after I've made her laugh with all that she is. I tell
her, "I miss my family, friends, good food,

even my mother's dog. I miss you too, of course."
She is gentle. She replies, "I bet that's so hard for you.

I would struggle." I am powerless. I want

to reach through my computer's screen, pull

her to me, promise, "I miss you most of all."

We are not a couple. Not anymore, after I have broken

both of our hearts in a half-assed attempt to protect hers

without needing to grow myself. But, I'm growing now.

I am stable. I miss someone I love.

# Poem in Which I Keloid

Grow on my hip, smooth and hairless

mass of tightly packed collagen. Cover

the incision and then some. Hide

the scalpel's handiwork. Precision is silent.

There is violence in the stillness of lying

on an operating table unconscious

and God knows I'm a victim.

I was not there for my muscle and sinew

to be stretched apart to make clean

my broken femur that was drilled into

turned into a dusty sponge. Three

screws to fill it in. The aftermath is ugly

a growth, benign yet jarring

hideous yet intriguing to run fingertips

over and trace the line of where I imagine

I was sliced open.

"The fracture is from repeated trauma.

The pounding of your foot on the pavement

you ran on, it was too much," the surgeon told

me with the sad joy he took in his job.


Is that what it is to be good?

To hate yourself for loving the shriek

a bone makes when a drill bit forces

its tongue in to mend bones

that ought not be broken?

Or is it to keloid?

# Poem in Which I Go Skiing

How I love to feel the feeling
of gliding on snow, skis
underfoot, jacket zipped snuggly,
goggles hugging tight like a memory
so they leave their ring imprinted
on my forehead and under
my eyes—the mark of snow angels—
but without wearing a face covering
so the wind can bite and burn
my youthful face, and my tongue
can taste snowflakes
at what must be ninety miles per hour,
and, for a moment, I live
in the impossible silence
of snow falling, swallowing
noise as I hurtle down a mountain
chasing my tranquil imagination.

# Poem in Which I Fall in Love

My Italian cologne smells like Frank Ocean on the beach.
The salt foam rushes through my pores

puffing me up like the balloons I bought for her birthday.
She laughs when I pretend to drown, wrapping her arms

around my chest, tugging on its hairs, kissing
the salt on my forehead. We lay in a hammock listening

to "Pink Matter." She is gentle, like Frank's voice
as he croons, *I close my eyes and fall into you.*

I have never been this close to someone before.
My fingertips trace pyramids on the small

of her back moving, nimbly as Andre's voice
over the electric guitar as he raps, *I need to hold your hand.*

They climb to her cheek nestled into my chest.
"You smell nice," she says.

I tell her I try to. I don't tell her I paid
seventy Euros in Ana Capri for this smell.

My Italian Cologne—*Carthusia Uomo.*
It smells like the gift of her body pressed against mine

on the back porch of her house on Kiawah Island
while her friends party inside and her mother sleeps.

We wake up to watch the sunrise the next morning.
I still have school. She just graduated.

*Carthusia Uomo.* Now, it smells like listening
to Frank Ocean in the airport as my sunglasses hide farewell.

# Poem in Which I am Temperate

I now prefer temperate spring to summer's heat.

It drenches me in my own sweat

and sticks my shirt to my back. I let

myself taste the honeysuckles' sweet

nectar in April. The autumn leaves comfort me.

Their colors, of the Earth's palette,

range from deep clays to October sunsets.

The world dies, turns gray by winter's freeze.

Still, I long for ice biting my back

before I dive into a burning hot spring.

Still, I cannot help but miss snowcone shacks

in the death heat of August. I must swing

in hammocks in late September to relax

my mind. So as the world gently turns, I sing.

# Poem in Which I Use My Skills Effectively

I wake up at six in the morning everyday to write,

read, and drink decaffeinated coffee for an hour. I watch

the Sun rise. Then, I practice gratitude. I really do.

I revise in the afternoons for an hour, when the day

is too hot to think, and sweat drips down my forehead

if I even sit outside for a moment. I really do.

When I'm distressed, I tell myself, "Breathe

if only for a moment." I can soothe myself now,

now that I am straddling stability. I really can.

Still, I miss mania.

Still, depression lulls me in.

In those moments, I take a deep breath, practice loving kindness,

remind myself, "I don't like it. That's okay. I can stand it anyway."

I really can. I really do.

# Acknowledgments

I'm eternally grateful to my family for their support through all of the stories behind these poems. I'd like to use this space to particularly acknowledge Chris Arvidson, Michele Poacelli, and Andrew McFadyen-Ketchum who have guided me through many stages of my writing journey. I'd also like to thank Ron Boudreaux, Jessica Hof, Brandon Andrus, Bryan Zitzman, Kurt Dunkel, Margot Brandi, Kevin Marra, Ryan Kelly, and any other mental health professional who has ever been a part of my team. Thanks to everyone I've met in treatment centers for helping me learn to be a better version of myself.

Lastly, I'd like to thank you, the reader, for putting in the emotional work required to read this book. Thank you for caring.

## LUTHER KISSAM V

Luther Kissam V studies English and creative writing at the University of North Carolina at Charlotte. He is an alumnus of Sewanee Young Writers' Conference and Kenyon College's Young Writers Summer Residential Workshop. He writes about aging neighbors and favorite rappers, and in this collection, resiliency while living with bipolar disorder. He is working on his first novel.

CPSIA information can be obtained at www.ICGtesting.com
Printed in the USA
BVHW041143130522
636969BV00005B/28